DARE TO DO IT Afraid

A COLLECTION OF
SHORT POEMS, QUOTES, AFFIRMATIONS AND ARTWORK

BY
GLYNIS T. EUGENE

DARE TO DO IT AFRAID

A COLLECTION OF
SHORT POEMS, QUOTES,
AFFIRMATIONS AND ARTWORK

By
Glynis T. Eugene
New Orleans, Louisiana

For written permission and/or additional information contact
Glynis T. Eugene via email at info@glyniseugene.com

ISBN: 979-8-218-00320-3 (Paperback)

Copyright Registered with Library of Congress

Cover photograph by Glynis T. Eugene
Front cover, back cover, book design and
artwork by the author, Glynis T. Eugene.

Printed in the United States

In memory of
Glenda & Quiana Eugene,
Krystal, Marion, & Cecelia,
and their fiery, daring spirits.

DEDICATION

This book is dedicated to my tribe.
Thank you for believing in me
and pouring your time and
encouragement into me.

To everyone who finds
themselves trapped in their
comfort zone, bound by fear
and doubt . . .

ACKNOWLEDGMENTS

To my
cousin Renee
and my
daughter Schwanna,
who have held my arms up,
my Aunt Gail
for those abrupt and deep
conversations,
this book would not exist if it
wasn't for each of you.

*Facing the fear
can be uncomfortable
but uncomfortable places
can be beautiful.*

glynis eugene

CONTENTS

Let your FAITH be BIGGER
than your fear!

Hebrews 13:6

FOREWORD

I admire Glynis as a person. She has remarkable talents, including deep imagination, detailed thinking, speaking, discernment, and dedication to listening attentively to others. She is an amazing woman of God. The opportunity to write this forward fills me with humility and elation. This is a great honor.

Glynis and I first met at The Upperroom Bible Church, where we served together with the greeters' ministry. I cannot remember how we started talking, but I knew she wanted to talk to me. We connected immediately. What God allowed me to see was Glynis' insecurities about herself. She did not know that. I did whatever necessary to help her address the issues. She was surprised by our conversation, and she became comfortable. As we grew closer, we began to talk on the phone for hours, discussing work, goals, dreams, visions, etc. We became an inspiration to each other.

Glynis is knowledgeable. One day, she called me with this lengthy conversation, precisely to ask me to be her mentor. I said, "Lord, as smart as this girl is, she still doesn't realize she is mentoring *me*. Open her eyes, please".

Insecurity is a demon that refuses to allow you to let go of anything that suffocates your purpose. If you are a person in bondage with others or yourself, feeling unstable, failure, or vulnerability, emotionally dependent, or avoid social interaction, I recommend *Dare To Do It Afraid*. My two favorite poems from this book are *Don't Dwell* and *Manifest*.

Dare To Do It Afraid is a masterpiece from God; where you will learn how to embrace rejection and not become easily offended. You will understand everything good to *you* is not good for you. *Dare To Do It Afraid,* will give you the authority, confidence, and boldness to take back your purpose that was stolen from you. You will understand your life from the perspective of Jesus Christ, by way of the Holy Spirit.

You do not have to do it alone. God says, "I am right here with you." Prepare for your date with the Father; declare the affirmations in this book to yourself for thirty days. It will change your thoughts forever. Psalm 45:1 declares, *"My heart overflows with a pleasing theme; I address my verses to the king; My tongue is like the pen of a ready writer."*

I place a great deal of value on *Dare To Do It Afraid,* because freedom is a choice. When people fear freedom, they get comfortable in bondage and can find reality hard to accept. "Make peace with the woman in the mirror and watch how your reflection changes," which is my favorite quote by Glynis Eugene.

. . . a *life* ruled by fear is a life half-lived.

INTRODUCTION

This book is a project born from conversing with God. He said, "Use what you already have in your hands."

Initially, I didn't get it. I questioned God. "What do you mean? I don't have anything in my hands."

As time progressed, God brought me to a collection of notebooks and graphic files I had tucked away. He quickened my spirit to put them in a short book. Again, I questioned God. "Who would want to read this?"

After a few days, I decided to trust God and take a leap of faith. I started organizing my writings, putting everything into a digital format. Halfway through the initial process, the devil showed up with daggers of negativity. Fear of failure, fear of rejection, doubt, insecurities, over thinking, and more started taking up prime residence in my head. While entertaining the negative thoughts, I began to hide and constantly question my abilities. Procrastination and perfectionism showed up as nooses around my neck, suffocating me. I was stuck sitting on the sideline of life as the devil played peek-a-boo with my dreams and future. This went on for months.

To defeat the fear that held me captive, I began praying and reflecting. I closed my ears to the negativity of my inner critic.

Then, armed with "God's Word," I began decreeing: *I can do ALL things through Christ Jesus, The Greater One lives in me, I take bold action no matter what,* and *I finish what I start.*

Next, I dared myself to do it afraid—finish the book. Along the way, I reminded myself that "done is always better than perfect." So, with patience and urgency I have completed:

"Dare To Do It Afraid"

A collection of short poems, quotes,
affirmations and digital artwork
by yours truly.

Enjoy!

...a well-lived *life* is filled with courageous moments.

POEMS

. . . keep that ablaze!
God doesn't want us to be
shy with his gifts, but
bold and loving and sensible.

2 Timothy 1:7

ONCE TORN

Torn like unwanted pages of a book,
freed from the covers that once held
her captive;

Thrown aside, cast into the wind,
exposed to the harsh elements of life.

Redefined by her journey,
she discovered her voice.

She now speaks words of truth and
triumph, unbound by the pages of
the past.

TEARS

The heart speaks words
spoken in tears, collected
in bottles that He caps with
His everlasting love.

Don't Dwell
—Author Unknown

Don't dwell on what might
have been or the chances
you have missed.

Or the lonely nights that lie between
the last time lovers kissed.

Don't grasp too hard the memory of
the things that never came.

The door that did not open or the
wind that killed the flame.

There is still time enough to live...
And time enough to try again.

Be Happy.

THE PROCESS

My love,
never forget that
"becoming" the you God sees
is a process that requires
faith, time, obedience
and patience.

WITHIN

Fire in the belly.
Insecurity is the smoke
that suffocates from within.

As silence speaks of
mistakes and regret,
fear whispers doubt.

It is the words of life, love
and light that loosens
the grips of this
darkness.

A Caregiver's Tears

Emotionally drained, tired of
fighting, her heart is bruised
by toxic behaviors.

She finds solace walking in the rain.

Raindrops hide her tears,
the sounds of thunder stifle
her wailing cries.

While walking in the rain,
she reflects, and releases the pain,
tapping into God's unfailing love.
There, she finds the strength to
forgive and carry on.

MINE THE HEART

Some treasures come in the form
of precious stones: diamonds,
rubies, sapphires . . .

Some treasures come in the form
of precious metals: silver, gold,
platinum . . .

These treasures are found when we
mine the earth.

Other treasures come buried in
struggle, hidden in the storms of life.

That beauty isn't discovered until
you mine the heart.

LIFE

Precious moments tangled in
the trilogies of life, cascading
across time, creating memories . . .

The beauty of vulnerability,
disguised by the complexities
of life;

Surreal truths, lessons learned,
stories of joy and pain, love lost,
and love found,

Bursting with emotions like
volcanic eruptions,
her soul filled with excitement,
she was no longer afraid to live.

Life became her muse.

LOOK WELL TO THIS DAY

—Anonymous Author
Inspired by Kalidasa, Sanskrit Poet, 5th Century

Look well to this day,
For it and it alone is life.
In its brief course,
Lie all the essence of your existence:

The Glory of Growth
The Satisfaction of Achievement
The Splendor of Beauty

For yesterday is but a dream,
And tomorrow is but a vision.
But today well lived makes every
yesterday a dream of happiness,
And every tomorrow a
vision of hope.

STIMULATE

Let imagination be
the aphrodisiac that
stimulates your thoughts,
as the mind
gently strokes the soul,
capturing the essence of self.

MANIFEST

Open your eyes to dream
without limitations.
No boundaries, no fear.

Dream what
seems impossible.

Close your eyes to see
past the heavens,
impossibilities becoming real;
the spirit realm,
manifesting in the natural.

For that which has been seen,
declare and set it in order
as you plan with purpose,
executing with divine intentions,
manifesting the promises.

MASTERPIECE

Same artist,
different masterpiece.
For every woman's soul is unique.

IMPERFECT BEAUTY

She cherishes the imperfections,
falling in love with her flaws,
knowing they are essential parts
of her being.

Hidden strength found in the
acceptance of herself.

Shattered pieces mended by
divine love. Peace and freedom she
has found,

Covered by grace, she is light;
beauty that illuminates from
within.

TAKE ME AS I AM

Take me as I AM.
My quirkiness, the mistakes,
the failures and the flaws,
my past, my present and
my future.

Take me as I AM.
My bald head,
my flip lips, and
wide hips.

Take me as I AM.
A diamond in the rough,
an ember glowing in the fire,
a shooting star interrupting
darkness.

Take me as I AM.
Constantly growing and evolving,

(continue)

becoming, a better me every day.
Don't try to contain me.

Take me as I AM.
Pray for me.
Protect me.
Provide for me.
Love me into submission.

Take me as I AM.
Erupting with passion and
purpose, loving fiercely.
A rare and priceless
treasure; a divine gift.

Take me as I AM.
And I will, willingly, give
you all of me.

SHE IS POETRY

She is poetry.
A creative being
of boundless
potential.
An expression of
life lived as art.

BALD WOMAN

She is self-assured
and fiercely resilient.
Her femininity is not
defined by hair.
Her crown is permanent.
Her beauty is undisguised.
Her confidence is contagious.
Her sex appeal is alluring.
Her presence is powerful.

Bald Woman

Her soul glows with
love and self-acceptance.
She recognizes her worth.
She has shed a thousand
skins to become the woman
she is today.

ESSENCE

A hue of beauty, kissed by the sun,
a glow that cannot be contained.
She radiates confidence and courage.

Curvaceously framed, gifted by the Creator.
Birthing nations, purpose, and
infinite intelligence.
Creating legacy.

She is the epitome of beauty,
grace, and strength.

Surrounded by the wisdom of
those who have gone before her,
she perseveres.

Thriving beyond adversity.
Heaven's DNA is coursing
through her veins.
She is royalty.

HER

She creates her own moments,
just as she dances to the beat
of her own drum.

Singing her own song,
vibrating with energy,
just as she dances
with freedom and triumph.

Heart-beat filled with harmony,
captivating the soul,
just as she writes
her own story, allowing
her truth to be told.

SHE IS FREE

Shedding hair and limited beliefs;

No longer trapped by the
stereotypes and taboos imposed
by society.

Peeling back the layers, facing
fears and insecurities, loving
herself, becoming comfortable
in her skin;

Self-acceptance is her cure.

Hands trembling, knees knocking,
doing it afraid, not allowing
alopecia to stop her,

Beauty redefined,
unapologetically living her truth;

(continue)

facing the world without hair,
She is free.

September Moon

With the sun as her muse
and the clouds gently caressing her
enchanted silhouette, her warm
amber glow seductively
illuminates the autumn sky,
revealing the beauty that resides in
her cratered imperfections.

IT'S A CHOICE

Sis,
it's a choice.
Don't allow
the clouds to
stop you from
experiencing
the sun.

SURRENDER

A sky filled with howling whispers,
Under the dusk of disappointment,
I closed my eyes and
SURRENDERED;
all of my being and thoughts,
me versus every version of me.

Letting go of the past,
I released years of conditioning,
buried under piles of unmet expectations.
Desperately wanting love,
I've learned to love myself.

In the moments of stillness
I'm statured in divine love,
here I've discovered peace and clarity,
the forever flex.

BEAUTY MARKS

Birthmarks, dimples, freckles,
gapped teeth, moles, and more,
flaws and imperfections . . .
No, my love—divine works of art
cascading the body as a
human canvas,
displaying masterful patterns,
abstract in form,
beauty that transforms,
authentic and raw,
first seen with the heart,
and then the eyes.

DREAM YOUR DREAMS

Dreams so vivid you can
hear them speak.
Dreams so bold you can
smell the aroma of
manifestation.
Taste your dreams,
ripe and sweet,
like the nectar of
a juicy peach.

BLOOM

Trapped in a prison of comfort,
the place where dreams are buried.

Afraid to venture out—break free!

Run to the unfamiliar.
Chase the unknown.

Root yourself deeply in the
garden of discomfort;
the soil is rich with
boundless possibilities.

Take up space with the
thrones and the roses.

Beauty can bloom in
uncomfortable places.

A Thank You Note

To my tribe:

For all the times I have been
afraid of my own light and
you encouraged me;

For all the times you allowed
me to borrow the confidence
you had in me;

For all the times you saw what
I could not see in myself—
my value, my worth,
my greatness, my creativity;

For all the times you poured
into me, asking for nothing
in return;

For all those times, I say . . .

QUOTES & THOUGHTS

*A wise man will
hear, and will increase
in learning;*

Proverbs 1:5

Allow faith and courage to be the
fuel that propels you beyond
the borders of fears.

If it's both terrifying and
amazing then you should
definitely pursue it

—*Erada Svetlana*

To know thyself is the
beauty of self-discovery.

Showing up as the
unapologetic version of yourself
inspires others to be themselves.

Life requires vulnerability.
Sometimes it will be
messy and uncomfortable, but in the
process, strength, confidence,
resilience, wisdom and wholeness
are being produced,
and that is beautiful.

Make peace with the woman in
the mirror and watch how your
reflection changes.

Capture life by living,
for in every new experience, your
"why" is being fulfilled.

Allow life's adventures to
leave you breathless, as you
dare to do it afraid.

There is
freedom and power in
simply being you.

Allow your authenticity
to color the world
around you.

There is no greater journey
than the one you must take
to discover the treasures that
have divinely and distinctively
been placed inside you.

One day she took a
stand, not allowing fear to hold
her back and she soared.

You develop courage and find
freedom when you face your fears
and conquer your insecurities.

Never trust your fears
because they don't know
your strength.

—*Athena Singh*

Dream big dreams with
an open mind and a
daring heart.

Be patient with yourself.
Failure is ok.
Growth isn't linear.
One step forward, three steps
backwards, every footstep
is a part of the journey.

Give yourself permission to live
without regret, basking in the
haven of divine grace.

Life is a journey of
experiences. Go explore
and discover *you*.

Opportunities are often
concealed as problems
or obstacles, wrapped in fear.
Consider it a gift and don't
let that stop you.
Take action, remembering
faith is force far greater than fear,
and done is always better than
perfection.

AFFIRMATIVE
POEMS

. . . and you shall
decree a thing and
it shall be established
unto you;

Job 22:28

HOW TO USE THESE AFFIRMATIVE POEMS

This section contains affirmative poems, some that remind each of us of key Biblical truths. They are not prayers nor are they meant to replace prayer.

Affirmative poems are tools that assist in programming and reprogramming the conscious and subconscious mind. This changes your mindset, improve your confidence, and help you overcome negative thoughts. But first, you must believe that words have the ability to change your life. Belief and mustard seed-faith are activators. Without these two, it doesn't work. You are trying to convince yourself of something you low-key think is a lie.

FYI: Faith without works is dead. [Faith is belief in action—what you believe and the corresponding actions you take as a result of what you believe.]

These types of affirmations strengthen your faith; assist you in taking on the challenges of the day, help you grow in self-love, and push past daily obstacles to accomplish your divine purpose and goals. Speaking and/or writing daily affirmations can help you create new, healthier beliefs and habits.

Confessing these affirmative poems out loud, daily, with passion and boldness from a believing heart, paired with corresponding actions—life changing. The more energy, faith, and positive feelings you put into these affirmative poems, the more effective they will be.

The subconscious mind needs you to envision your desired outcome(s) in full-color with vivid imagination, imitation and intention. Remember, we become the reality of the words we speak. That's manifestation.

Now, let's start boldly confessing!

AFFIRM

I AM loved.

I AM worthy.

I AM valuable.

I matter.

I AM capable.

I AM enough.

I AM safe.

I AM overflowing with joy.

I AM investing in myself.

I AM learning, growing and
achieving my goals.

I AM optimistic
and thankful for this new day
and it's opportunities.

I AM living a life of purpose
and happiness.

I AM manifesting
the life of my dreams.

COURAGE

With a spirit of
power, love and a sound mind
I conquer fear.
With confidence, courage, boldness,
and divine assurance
I take on every challenge.
Daily, I AM moving beyond my
comfort zone, allowing
curiosity and growth to push me.
With courage, I AM creating positive
change in my life.
I stand firm in faith conquering
fear with action.
I AM called to show up.
I AM a risk taker.
With courage and spontaneity
I try new things,
even when it's uncomfortable.
I AM unstoppable.

EXPANSION

With a deep breath,
I inhale the essence of life,
exhaling every vain imagination.
I let go of all behaviors and habits
that don't serve my greatest good.
I release all limiting beliefs:
poverty, lack, doubt, procrastination,
disappointment, limitation, over-thinking,
comparison, and fear.
I AM making room for growth.
I AM evolving and prospering.
I AM increasing in my health,
and well-being.
My faith is expanding.
My territory is expanding.
My circle of influence is expanding.
I AM a magnet for billion dollar ideas.
I AM an instrument of infinite expansion
and love in the earth.

GUIDANCE

My footsteps are divinely ordered.
I trust the process during
the peaks, the valleys
and the detours
in my life.
I trust that everything
always works out for my
highest good.

HEALTH

I flow in divine health, healing
and wisdom every day.
My mind, body and spirit exist in
divine-alignment, harmony and peace.
Every cell, artery, vein, tissue, and organ,
systems in my body functions the way
God intended.
Sickness and disease are far from me.
I AM my ideal weight.
I eat right, drink enough water,
exercise, and get adequate rest.
I AM confident, enthusiastic
and energized.
I AM healthy and whole.
I look good and I feel great.

THE HEART

I release the fear of failure,
rejection and limited beliefs.
The peace of God which surpasses
all understanding, guards my
heart and mind.
With diligence and perseverance,
I keep my heart, for it is
the source of life.
My heart is filled with gratitude.
My heart and mind are filled
with loving, healthy, positive
and prosperous thoughts.

IMPACT

I AM
here to impact humanity in
profound ways, using my
gifts, talents, unique
creativity and life experiences.
I AM thankful for my capacity to
add value to other people's lives.

People around the world are being
helped by what I have to say and
the products and services I provide.
I AM leaving a positive and inspiring
mark in the hearts of every person
I come in contact with.

INFINITY

I AM
an unlimited being filled
with creative ideas, thoughts,
and infinite possibilities.
I AM full of divine-infinite value.
My creativity is always in demand.
My potential to succeed is infinite.
God's infinite wisdom,
plans, purpose and promises are
being demonstrated daily
in my life.

PROSPERITY

Favor abounds in my life.
My prosperity is inevitable.
Everything I touch prospers.
Doors of opportunity, increase and
expansion are open to me.
I honor The Greater One with all I have.
My life is overflowing with blessings.
Wealth and riches are in my house.
I have all sufficiency in every
area of my life.
I AM surrounded by abundance.
I AM an asset.
I AM paid well for being me.
I AM a giver. Therefore, I receive.
I manage my time, talents
and money well.
I AM wise with how I earn,
invest, grow and save.
Money flows into my life constantly
with ease, in increasingly large amounts
regardless if I work for it or not.

SELF-LOVE

Phenomenal by divine design,
I AM unconditionally loved.
Chosen by the Almighty,
fearfully and wonderfully made.
I AM the Apple of God's eye.
Greatness is in my DNA.
I AM worthy and deserving of the
best— nothing is too good for me.

My self-love is on repeat.
I love me!
I love myself out loud.
I love myself unconditionally.
I make no apologies for being the most.

I value every version of me.
I thank myself for choosing me.
I AM committed to my non-negotiables.
I take responsibility for
my own happiness.

(continue)

I hype myself up:
I love me!
I believe in me. I accept me.
I take up space, existing as I AM.
Love is always flowing to me.
No one who encounter me
is ever the same.
Babe — my presence is a Vibe!

I stay prayed up.
Daily I shine.
I AM an ever present blessing.
I surpass the norms.
I AM an oasis of positivity and joy.
I radiate love, certainty,
confidence and excellence.
My life is overflowing with
peace, love, purpose and abundance.

Just as I AM right now
— *I AM Enough.*

SPEAK

Life and death are in my mouth.
Therefore, I choose to speak life.
My words are powerful.
I AM intentional and effective with the
words I think, speak and write.
My words paint pictures.
I AM creating the life of my dreams
with my words and actions.
My deepest desires are
manifesting NOW!

VICTORY

Victory is mines.

I always triumph.

HE has set me on the path of

greatness, victory and divine destiny.

I AM the head and not the tail.

I AM above and not beneath.

I AM more than a conqueror.

No weapon formed against me

shall prosper.

I rule and reign in life.

I AM victorious.

With gratitude, and thankfulness

I experience victory,

every day in every way,

in all aspects of my life.

WEALTH

I AM wealthy.
I have a wealthy mindset.
I attract wealth beyond money.
God gives me richly all things to enjoy.
I AM overflowing in
infinite-value, wealth, and opulence.
I bask in the lap of luxury.
With gratitude I thankfully accept
the unlimited abundance and wealth
that has been laid up for me.
I AM creating generational wealth
and provision for my children's, children.
I AM impacting the community
with my wealth.
I AM the lender, not the borrower.
I give into every good work.
I AM living a life filled with time freedom
and financial freedom.

WHO I AM

I AM
a divine creation,
made in His image.
A masterpiece,
my ancestors' wildest dreams.
I AM freedom.
I AM hope.
I AM confidence.
I AM resilience.
I AM creativity.
I AM wealth.
I AM change.
I AM both the seed and the tree.
I have within me everything
I need to fulfill my destiny.

WISDOM

Rooted in wisdom from above,
grounded in the spirit of truth,
I AM emotionally, mentally,
physically and spiritually
stable and strong.
I AM calm and at peace.
I AM walking and growing in
wisdom, and discernment.
I hear from heaven.
I have clarity in all I do.
My steps are divinely ordered.
The Greater One gives me the words to speak.
I make wise and decisive decisions.
With gratitude, joy and thankfulness
I accept divine wisdom.

ABOUT THE AUTHOR

Glynis T. Eugene, a native New Orleanian, the owner of The Graphix Parlour, LLC, and GE Enterprises, LLC. Glynis is a graduate of Tulane University SCS with a B.A. in Social Science and an A.A. in Business. In addition, she has a A.A.S. in Computer Information Science from DeKalb Technical College.

As an entrepreneur, speaker, writer and multi-passionate creative, Glynis is driven by her commitment to inspire and impact humanity. She is passionate about encouraging women to connect with their authentic selves, live confident lives, step outside their comfort zones, embrace the NOW, and not wait to have new experiences.

WRITERS' CREDITS

Glynis Eugene   pages *4, 5-7, 10, 11, 13, 14, 16, 18, 19, 21, 22, 23, 24, 26-27, 28, 29, 31, 32, 33-34, 35, 36, 37, 39, 41 43, 45, 46, 48, 50-60, 62-67, 69-86*

Author Unknown pages *12, 20*
Erada Svetlana   pages *49*
Athena Singh   pages *61*

PHOTO/ARTWORK CREDITS

Glynis Eugene   pages *9, 11, 15, 17, 23, 25, 28, 30, 34, 35, 38, 40, 42, 44, 53, 56, 59, 67,*

LIKENESS PERMISSIONS

All likeness used with permission

Judy Dixon   Felictia Keys
Sharon Riley   Gail Eugene
Renee Gray   Monique Hagan

SCRIPTURE REFERENCES
King James & New International Versions

Genesis *1:26-27*	Proverbs *18:21*
Exodus *4:12*	Proverbs *22:7*
Leviticus *19:13*	Ecclesiastes *11:2*
Deuteronomy *8:18*	Isaiah *54:17*
Deuteronomy *14:2*	Jeremiah *29:11*
Deuteronomy *15:6*	Habakkuk *2:2-3*
Deuteronomy *28:3-14*	Luke *6:38*
Deuteronomy *30:8-10*	Luke *10:7*
Joshua 1:8	Luke *12:12*
1 Chronicles *4:10*	John *3:16*
Job *22:28*	John *4:10*
Psalm *17:8*	John *14:17*
Psalm *37:4*	John *15:4-5*
Psalm *37:23*	Romans *8:28*
Psalm *112:3*	Romans *12:6-8*
Psalm *139:14*	Romans *8:31-39*
Proverbs *1:5*	1 Corinthians *10:13*
Proverbs *4:22-23*	2 Corinthians *2:14*
Proverbs *13:22*	2 Corinthians *9:8*
Proverbs *16:3*	2 Corinthians *10:5*

SCRIPTURE REFERENCES
King James & New International Versions

Ephesians *1:18-20*	James *2:26*
Philippians *4:7-8*	1 Peter *2:9-10*
1 Timothy *1:14*	1 Peter *4:10*
1 Timothy *6:17*	1 John *4:4*
2 Timothy *1:7*	1 John *5:4*
Hebrews *13:6*	Revelation *5:10*
James *1:5*	Ephesians *3:20*

faith over fear
dare to do it
afraid

Made in the USA
Coppell, TX
27 September 2022

83657065R10062